The Ugly Duck of Atlanta

A VERY TRUE STORY

Jerome Carithers

Atlanta, GA

All rights reserved. No part of this publication may be reproduced or transmitted for commercial purposes, except for brief quotations, without written permission of the publisher.

ISBN-13: 9798867828653

Copyright©2023

Jerome Carithers

SevenWiseMen82@gmail.com

List of Episodes

Episode 1

- Let me introduce myself

In a world of many different colors of people, my skin hue was called red, yellow, light skinned, white boy, blue blood, and black. What a mess for me! I was too black to be called white and too white to be called black.

Hello, my name is Jerome Carithers. I was born March 1st, 1947, at Grady Memorial Hospital in Atlanta, Georgia. Not the Grady that is standing now, but old Grady that used to sit across the street from where the new building is standing now. If you were born back in the mid 40's to late 50's, you probably know what I'm talking about.

In 1947 the average income was about $3,000 a year, Jackie Robinson was the first black baseball player in the major leagues who broke the color barrier, and it was the beginning of the cold war between America and the Soviet Union. I was known as what some people called a love child. This is a child, girl, or boy, that is born out of wedlock.

My biological father was named Tommy Lee Webb, my mother was Dorothy Carithers. She ended up marrying a man by the name of Jack Kelly when I was about five years of age. He was a truck driver. Mother went to school and became a nurse. I had two other brothers and one sister. My family and friends say that I look like my mother.

I was raised up on the east side of Atlanta. DeKalb was my county. My settlement was called Edgewood, a small community where everybody knew each other. My mother was born in Florida. My biological father was born in Atlanta, Georgia, but my stepfather was born in Covington, Georgia, about 35 miles out of Atlanta. My grandfather's name was Gus Carithers. This is where our family name came from. We simply called him Gus. My mother said Gus was half Cherokee Indian, and was born in Social Circle, GA. She told me a story of how Gus would wash his long black hair in dish water for the minerals that came from the water. Imagine that.

As far back as I can remember, I was in the kindergarten at Westland Avenue Elementary School. My teacher was named Miss Starling. She was a very pretty lady, easy on your eyes.

It was in the kindergarten that I realized I had an unusual last name. To this very day, people have trouble with pronouncing it. Some of my teachers even had a problem with the pronunciation of Carithers. I would get embarrassed each time it was called. My friends made fun of it all the time, especially in school. I was bullied a lot of times because of it in and out of school. I believe that this is how my fighting started in my early years. My parents and my siblings still say to this very day in life that if you make fun of my name, then the fight would be on like popcorn!

As a young boy, most of my corporal punishment came from being at the dinner table. Breakfast, that was not a problem, but at dinner time I could not eat what my parents and my other siblings would eat. I was just different. No squash for me. No pig ears for me. No chicken feet for me.

No collard greens for me. No "chitlins" for me. No okra for me . . .just to name to few.

To this day I have always tried to be a clean and neat person. No dirt under my fingernails, my hair had to be combed, and my shoes had to be shined. I was the oddball of all my siblings. I was always different.

For some strange reason I just had a problem fitting in. One of the reasons was because of my skin color. It was like a dirty red. My two brothers and my one sister were darker than I was, and they thought that I thought that I was better than they were, but that was not the case. I have always had the innate feeling of doing the right thing even though I got in a lot of fights in my early childhood.

From my many fights along with my skin color, my nickname was Dirty Red. That was also my biological father's nickname. At a very early age I realized that I liked church and Sunday school. Of the two, it was Sunday school for me. My teacher was named Miss Boxdale, who at that time was a small, tiny lady who also played the piano and was dubbed as the church pianist.

My first Pastor was named Reverend E. D. Thomas. He was a large man, very tall, and walked with a limp. He was what you may call a fire and brimstone preacher. The name of the church was Beulah Baptist Church. It sat on the corner of Wesley Avenue and Hardee Street. In the settlement, or community called Edgewood, my school and my church were only blocks apart. My parents and my siblings all went to a church called Travelers Rest, and the other church was called Antioch. This is where they went to church. I would get up every Sunday morning and walk to Beulah by myself.

Back in those days we had no Middle school, so we went from the 7th grade to high school. Imagine that. The principal at Wesley Avenue School was Sammye Cohen. She was about 4 feet nothing, but she was rough and took no stuff.

Back in the fifties and early sixties, we only had five black high schools that we could go to. They were Carver, Archer, Turner, Washington

High School, and David T Howard High School and that was it. Now, back to Sunday school.

I believe I joined Beulah at the age of about eleven or twelve. The church was a two-story structure made of wood and brick, but mostly wood. I loved my church and the Sunday school.

My first little job was also in my neighborhood. It was one block away from the church. I worked in a grocery store called Pollard's. This was around 1957 or 1958. I was around 10 or 11 years of age. My job was to carry the customers' groceries to their cars and sometimes to their homes. If they did not have a car, I would carry them with my two feet.

I remember in the community of Edgewood we had what I called The Rag Man. He came around once or twice a week to buy cheap old clothes. He had a very large wooden cart that he would push around on two wheels. He had a weight scale and a cow bell and would sing his jingle . . . "Come on everybody it's the Rag Man", over and over again, "It's the Rag Man". He would give you fifty cents for a pound of old clothes. How about that y'all?

Also in the fifties, roller skating was very popular, especially on Christmas Day. We would skate from Atlanta to the city of Decatur. What a thrill it was for all of us! It would be about 15 or 20 of us, girls, and boys, mostly boys. Back in the day, there were two types of roller skates, union hardware and flyaways, sometimes called pipes.

The union hardware was the cheapest of the two, you had to work your legs and feet very hard for them to roll fast, and we also had to cut tire inner tube rubber from bicycles to make the skates stay on your feet. But the pipes, or flyaways was a different story. The flyaways skates rolled much faster with much less work, and they cost more money. We would put long ascots in our back pockets and off to Decatur we would go.

In the summer months for vacation, I would stay with my cousin Zike. He would introduce me as an Edgewood bully. The more fights I won, the less fights I had, so it was advantageous for me to win.

Also in the fifties, Monday, Tuesday, Wednesday, Thursday, Friday, and Saturday was business as usual in the south, but on Sunday all businesses would be closed out of respect for God and the Blue Law. All grocery stores and all service stations would be closed. You would have to get your gas and groceries no later than Saturday night. Imagine that if you can.

Also back in those days, we had a Big Red, or the Trolley System. At that time, it was called Atlanta Transit instead of Marta which it's called today. The bus was powered by electricity that ran off electrical cable wires that were located on the top of the bus. I believe the cost of the bus ride was ten cents. Oh, my how times have changed! Can you imagine all of the merchant's businesses that closed on Sunday, like Chick-fil-A does today?

At the age of twelve, I became a door-to-door sales representative for a black magazine called Jet. Jet is the first magazine that I ever saw with all black faces. At that time, these small magazines cost about fifteen cents per copy. I believe I got a nickel for every copy I sold.

I saved enough nickels to buy my first pair of shoes, they were called wing tips. I admired them very much. The bed that I slept on was called a rollaway bed. It was a metal frame that folded in the center and was supported by small metal springs, and it would have a mattress that matched the springs and the bed size. This bed set very close to the floor, so after shining my shoes, I would fall asleep admiring my pretty wing tip shoes.

As I can recall, my first barber was named Mister Ralph. He was a very unique barber in the fact that he would place you down in his chair, then he would light his cigarette, but he would never puff it. The ash from the cigarette never fell off until he was through with your haircut. Then he would say, "Next" and he would then puff the cigarette when he was through cutting your hair. I believe the cigarette ash was his timer for how long he would stay on a head of hair to be cut.

When I was about five years old, there was a breakfast cereal called Sugar Jets. It was my favorite. It was very, very sweet. After watching several commercials about this cereal, they convinced me that when I ate the cereal, I would be able to fly. So, one day I made a cape out of one of my old long sleeve shirts. I tied it around my neck and jumped off our back porch, which was about seven feet high, and oh boy was I surprised . . . I could not fly. The only thing I got after eating the cereal was a sprained ankle. I found out the hard way that Sugar Jets could not make me fly!

Even as a young boy, I liked nice clothes and nice shoes. My mother used to tell me stories about my biological father. He was quite the ladies' man and loved clothes also. Maybe that's why I like fresh, clean clothes. But I never liked sneakers or tennis shoes. To this very day, they always make my feet smell.

I believe that I was about six years of age when I decided that I wanted to be a Cub Scout, so I joined. I really enjoyed becoming a scout. I loved wearing that beautiful blue and gold uniform. As life would have it, that blue and gold would come again later in my years in high school. What was amazing to me about the Cub Scouts was they had secret handshakes and secret codes. I learned how to mark a trail in case you got lost. The markings would show you how to get back. All these things were new and very exciting to me. We were given a handbook to learn. The value of becoming a scout, giving honor to God, being morally straight, and obeying the laws of the pack.

At the age of about nine, I got myself a little job with the Atlanta Journal and Constitution delivering newspapers. Of course, it was during the summer months while school was not open. The Constitution paper was the morning paper, the Journal was the evening paper. I threw the Journal, which was the evening paper. My route was about a mile and a quarter, and yes, I walked five days a week carrying that big white canvas bag on my shoulder. I would pick up my bundles of newspapers at the corner of Mason Avenue and Boulevard Drive which is now Hosea Williams Drive. That pile of papers would be in front of Dr. Douthard's house. He was the first black doctor that my eyes had ever seen.

I recall one day I went to pick up my bundles of newspaper. On this day, one of the neighborhood bullies decided that he was going to take my papers away from me. I was so overwhelmed by this big teenager that I left the scene right away. I went and got my big cousin Tommy who came to my defense. One of my favorite quotes reads, "He who walks away, lives to fight another day". Tommy gave this big bully about ten choice words that were not nice words to say, if you get my meaning y'all. And that big bully left in a New York minute - quick, fast, and in a hurry! And I resumed with my paper route each day.

When I was about halfway through my paper route, I would stop at one of the corner stores and buy me a soda pop. We called them drinks. The name of this soda pop, or drink, was Topper Cola. It was a very large soda pop that my dad nicknamed the belly washer. I would also buy myself cookies. We called them twofers because you'd get two cookies for a penny. Now, back to my elementary school, Wesley.

Our principal was named Sammye Cohen. The name Sammy usually refers to a man, but in this case, Sammye was a woman. I spent a lot of time in her office for fighting and cursing about my skin color and my last name, Carithers. Miss Cohen was only about 4 feet and some change. She had what we call today a short person syndrome. Miss Cohen said what she meant and meant what she said. She was a very strict lady. After her retirement, the school was named after her. The Sammye E. Cohen Middle School in Atlanta, Georgia.

When I was in the fourth or fifth grade, my teacher was named Miss Bronner. One day she asked the class what a woodchuck is. All of my classmates gave the same answer, but not me. I was so afraid. I was actually frightened, and I had a very eerie feeling about it, but I kept my answer. I kept holding on to faith and as it turned out, I was the only student at that time that got the answer correct. This turned out to be a lifelong lesson for me, sometimes you can be the only one that's right. I found out later on in life that Miss Bronner was one of the siblings of The Bronner Brothers, a very famous black hair product company. Their products are still on the market today.

When I was about the age of nine years old, my parents moved us from Hutchinson Street in Edgewood to Amenda Street, also located in Edgewood. The apartments were about two miles apart from each other. It was during this time that I met Rev. S. T. Huff. He was the leasing manager for the apartments where my family moved to.

Episode 2

- Meeting Rev. Huff

Out of maybe 200 girls and boys, Rev. Huff chose me to be his little helper. I believe there were twice as many kids as adults on the grounds of the leasing office. The first time I saw a person make it rain, it was Rev. Huff. He would go to the bank every Friday and get twenty dollars' worth of change in dimes, pennies, quarters, nickels, one-dollar bills, and there was one coin called fifty cent which the government took out of circulation years later.

He would put all the change in a brown paper bag and throw a handful at a time. When that change hit the ground, the fighting, the scratching, the kicking, and knockdowns all happened. After I would receive about seventy-five cents worth of change, I'd be satisfied. The last money that he would throw to us would be a dollar bill wrapped around a fifty-cent piece. By me being a small boy, after I got my seventy-five-cent quota, I would be through with all the fighting, scratching, kicking, getting knocked down, and stomped on. I would go to the back of the crowd and look very sad and pathetic. I would hold my head down and cross my legs and look as pitiful as I possibly could. Then he would pretend he was going to throw to the left and then to the right and all the kids would go to the left and then to the right. I stayed in my spot, and he would always throw me the fifty-cent piece wrapped up in the dollar bill. That's how our beautiful relationship got started and I became his little helper.

Part of my job was to deliver late notices to the residence of the apartments, help out around the office, sweep the floors, and do little odds and ends for him. One weekend Rev. Huff called my mother and asked her if he could take me to church with him and his wife, and she gave her permission.

Rev. Huff was a United Methodist Pastor. His wife was an Atlanta public school teacher. Rev. Huff had bought me a pair of Buster Brown shoes. Back in those days, Buster Brown was a very nice and very expensive shoe. It had a little bulldog on the label of the shoe and his name was Tige. When you saw that label, that's when you knew you had a pair of genuine Buster Brown shoes.   Rev. Huff was a very compelling human being. I think I believed every word he said.

There were two large apartment complexes in Edgewood, the red complex, and the white complex. We were always at war, the red against the white, and we were fighting a lot. If you lived in the white complex, it was not in your best interest to stay in the red for very long.

When I reached about the sixth grade, I would meet a young boy by the name of Roy Ward. He and I were always against the white apartment complex. One year our parents bought us Red Ryder BB guns for Christmas. We would challenge the white complex with our bb guns, never thinking about the consequences of our behavior.

Incidentally, these two complexes were called red or white because of their color being all white or all red. In reference to Rev. Huff, God would reveal some of his secrets, or angels to you even as a child. At some point in time, my family moved out of the red complex, and I lost contact with Rev. Huff until I became a full-grown man. Now on to yet another episode.

Episode 3

- My best friend, Blue

My best friend Roy E. Ward, aka Blue, and I entered the seventh grade together. Back in the late fifties the Atlanta public schools did not have what we call middle school today. The seventh grade was the highest grade you could achieve in elementary school and there were only five high schools that Blacks could attend throughout the city of Atlanta. They were Carver High School, Turner High School, Washington High School, Archer High School, and Howard High School. Because of our location in the community, we were selected to go to David T. Howard High School which was the closest to us.

I could always count on Blue in good times and bad times. My mother said that if you ever find one friend in life, you are blessed. Our nicknames were Red and Blue of course because of our color.

Blue was very dark skinned and when he got angry, his eyes turned red, and he would be ready to fight.

Now he and I are off to high school. If you can recall earlier in my story about the blue and gold colors of the Cub Scouts, well, those just happened to be the colors of my high school, David T. Howard High. Imagine that y'all. Our mascot was a ram. We were the MIGHTY, MIGHTY RAMS.

Around 1961 or 62, my family and I moved to a community or settlement called Reynoldtown. This community was built between 1960 and 1969. Reynoldtown is bordered on the west by Pearl Street. Another settlement was called Cabbagetown. Two very close communities.

Reynoldtown was mostly populated by African Americans and Cabbagetown was populated by white or Anglos, or hillbillies by birth. Cabbagetown was not a good place for a Black person to be caught in day or night. Cabbagetown had a cotton mill in the center of their small community.

Although my memory is not as vivid as it once was, I can remember on several occasions while riding the Atlanta bus system, or transit system as it was called at that time and not MARTA. Black men and Black women would board the bus at the Krog Street tunnel in Cabbagetown. They would have cotton in their hair and an odor that would say I have had a very long night! So, I learned at a very early age that I did not want this job. I dared not to miss the bus to school, or it would be a long walk, about four miles.

On one occasion, I missed the school bus. I remember that day. It was ten degrees that morning. The wind was blowing very hard as I made that four mile walk to the school. Once I arrived, I was told by one of the teachers that the steam heater had stopped working and I realized that I would have to make that four mile walk all over again. That was some morning for me. I said to myself that I would always remember that morning for the rest of my life. No girls for me to see that day, what a shame.

While I attended my high school, I never had an attendance problem, especially when I found out that was where all the girls were. It was like a merry-go-round for me. Every time I thought I saw a pretty girl, I would look again, and I'd find one even prettier.

It was in high school that I learned to shoot dice, or craps. Some people call it the game of chance. I believe I shot dice from the eighth grade to the twelfth. I was also cutting a lot of classes. On one occasion while I was cutting class, I got caught by Mr. Harris. While I was down on my knees trying to make my point, he walked into the boy's bathroom. None of the other boys told me that he was standing right behind me. He said to me, "Son, you're supposed to be in my class." My eyes got big as golf balls. Blue was long gone, and all of the other guys were too. Well, that stopped my class cutting days at Howard High.

Blue and I loved football, and the girls loved the players, so Blue and I became football players. Blue made the team as a lineman, and I made the team as a running back at only 147 pounds. When we practiced after school each day, I got beat up a lot. There was one time a lineman, who weighed about 350 pounds, hit me so hard that my hip pads were turned around to the other side. The coach asked me, "Son, are you ok?" I said, "I think I need a water break right now."

During football season, the school would give the team what we called a pep rally in the school gymnasium before every game. Our old gym would be rocking to cheer the team on. We were the MIGHTY, MIGHTY RAMS! When the players would be introduced over the microphone one by one, there would be pandemonium. There was so much excitement and love for our players. When we played our archrivals, some of our players would go to the woodshop in school and make a casket with the name of the opposing team on it, the Washington High Bulldogs, to let everyone know what we were going to do to those Bulldogs. We were like pall bearers carrying the bodies of our opponents.

I had a hard time in the classes that I attended at David T. Howard High. I was not a fast learner. I struggled to get a C average, and I had a lot of help from loving teachers who were there to guide me. I take this time out now to thank them. My homeroom teacher was Miss G. Abercrombie.

She was fine on the outside and fine on the inside if you get my point. If she had only known how much in love I thought I was with her LOL.

In 1960, students came from all over the city of Atlanta. My class was the largest class that ever attended David T. Howard High with 790 students strong. From elementary school to high school was quite a transitional change for me, new friends, and new acquaintances.

It was in the early sixties that I would meet Walter Frazier on the football field. He was our quarterback. He was also our point guard on the basketball team. His nickname was Clyde until he was playing for the New York Knickerbockers. He went on to become one of 50 of the greatest players ever to play the game, according to the NBA aka National Basketball Association.

One day in my spelling class, I remember the teacher asking me to spell pneumonia. My response was "n-e-w-m-o-n-i-a". She said, "No Carithers, try again". I said, "n-e-w," she said, "the way it's spelled is p-n-e-u-m-o-n-i-a," and my reply was, "Oh, I thought you said newmonia not permonia". It was obvious to the teacher and the class that I did not study at all. The joke was on me LOL.

When I used to cut class a few years earlier at D. T. H. High, we put a hole at the end of a fence and covered it with a brown wooden board. You could see a student standing at the end of the fence, and all of a sudden that student would disappear or vanish or pass from sight. That student went through the hole in the ground.

If my memory serves me correctly, I was a sophomore when I got into one of my hobbies again, fighting. This time it was over a girl. She was in the tenth grade. She was very pretty to look at. Her name was Pat. The other boy and I were fighting over the same girl. We were dating the same girl at the same time. Imagine that if you will. Maybe some of you boys can testify.

This fight happened on Auburn Avenue, a very popular street in Atlanta. We got into an argument in front of Haugabrooks Funeral Home. The argument turned into a fight. My Mom had just bought me a new shirt. It was torn to pieces and my friend James came by and stopped the fight. Boy was I glad he came by. As I began to walk away from the fight with my back turned to the other guy, he was charging at me with a big red brick, not a rock. A friend of mine named Albert knocked the brick out of his hand and saved me from serious harm.

It was at David T. High that I would meet my first wife. Her name was Kate. She had very long hair and was very pretty, easy on the eyes to look at. Guess what? It was Blue who gave her a note that I had written for him to give to her. It was in social studies that I asked Blue to pass this note to this pretty young girl, and I guess it worked.

Some of the most prominent people that attended David T. Howard High School were Martin Luther King Jr. He was one of America's greatest civil rights leaders of all time. Maynard Holbrook Jackson, who was the first black mayor for the city of Atlanta at the age of 35. The name of our airport was Hartsfield International Airport, but because of Maynard Jackson's contributions to our city, and his help with the airport, the name was changed to Hartsfield Jackson International Airport. A lot of history came out of old D. T. H. High School. Like Clarence Cooper, a very well-known judge here in Atlanta, Police Chief Elgin Bell for the City of Atlanta, and the list goes on.

Before class would start, every morning in our homeroom we would all gather in back of the coat room. The girls and boys would all sing doo-wop songs. An example would be "You Lied...You cheated, you lied, you said that you loved me..." a song by The Slades. We would sing and dance to the music of James Brown, Jackie Wilson, Jerry Butler, and of course the queen of soul, Aretha Franklin. Boy did we have a lot of fun in those days.

The road that I have traveled in my young life was not easy, but some unknown spirit was always with me and covering me. The last confrontation that I had in high school was about my skin color. This time, a gang of boys were waiting for me at my normal bus stop. I was about one block away from that bus stop when I saw these guys waiting for me. Now remember, one of my favorite quotes is, he who walks away lives to fight another day, so on that day...that particular day, I went to another bus stop. LOL!

Even as a child I had some experience with racial discrimination here in the city of Atlanta. In the late 1950's and early 60's, a black police officer could not arrest a white man or a white woman. The black officer would have to hold them until a white police officer arrived at the scene of the crime. Public bathrooms had signs on the outside saying "White only". Public water fountains, "White only". Swimming pools and many more public facilities were segregated.

I remember when I was a small boy watching all the white kids swimming. The only thing that I could do was look at them. I wasn't light skinned enough to swim at that park. LOL. The Park was called Candler Park. It was named after Asa Griggs Candler, the Coca Cola magnate.

Candler Park is very rich in history. It was once called Edgewood in 1890. It was a very nice neighborhood for some people to raise a family. Let me share another episode with y'all.

Episode 4

- One big bully

When football season would be over, then it was basketball season. One Friday night, my amigos and I were at a basketball game. A big bully came into the boy's bathroom at half time while James, Blue and me were drinking out of one tall can of beer.

All of a sudden, this big bully snatched the can out of my hand. He was about 270 pounds and was about 6'2"! WOW! So, I looked up at him and I said, "Ok big man, you win."

Come that next Friday at the game, at the same location, I said to James and Blue, "I'm going to fix that big bully." I urinated in that beer can before he arrived. Then he came in and repeated that act again. He turned the can up and drank the entire contents of the can and then he said to me, "Now I'm drunk." LOL. Wow.

The moral of this story is, never take what does not belong to you. Here is another episode.

Episode 5

- Waltzing thru my Junior Year

I remember that I was an escort at the inaugural ball. Most of the football players were chosen for that event. Our queen was being introduced to the student body for the first time. They escorted the queen and her court. We all had to learn how to do a dance called the waltz. The waltz is a ballroom and folk dance. It was my first time wearing a tuxedo. Our Queen was one of the prettiest girls in the city of Atlanta.

I don't remember a whole lot about my junior year in high school, but on one occasion after the prom was over, my mom had given me only $5.00 to spend after the dance was over. At that time, I was dating a young girl from Washington High School, not Howard, but Washington High, our archrivals.

On this particular night, we went to what we called the Split-T out on Simpson Road in Atlanta.

It was a very well-known eating establishment. The servers would bring your food on a tray and put it on your car window. Once he placed our food on the window, my window fell out! LOL! What an embarrassing moment for me but I was determined not to let this young lady convince me to spend the whole $5.00! LOL.

Other than that, my junior year went by pretty fast, like a flash. Basically, we were all getting ready for our senior year, our final year in high school. Unfortunately for me, in my senior year, my pelvic bone was cracked one day during football practice. It was the end of my career. But on the other hand, my team, the mighty, mighty Rams of David T. High School, for the first time in the school's history, won the city, the state, and the regional championships. What a team! It was such a thrill. There was so much excitement for the whole school.

Our class graduation of 1965 was upon us. Our graduation was held at the City Auditorium in downtown Atlanta on Courtland Street. If you were in the audience that night, the chairs were arranged so that they looked like the number 65. What an awesome sight. The 65 represented the year that we graduated. Dreadfully on that night we lost two classmates, Jacob Hamon and Luther Hughey. They lost their lives while changing their car tire. They were hit by another passing car. Sad but true.

Now that I had graduated, I did not know what my first move would be. I guess that's how a baby bird felt when it was put out of the nest for the first time. My very first real job was working on the production line at a shoe manufacturing company called Genesco Shoes. It was a wonderful feeling to have my own money in my pocket. My particular job was called a side-laster. It involved the process of laying down the leather of the shoe and forming a heel pattern. I had to pack a nail on the inside of the left side, and the right side of the heel part of the shoe.

Salary was based on production. Production would determine, on a weekly basis, how much money that you would make from each piece job that was performed. I was so fast at my job that I would have production at 12 each day. I'd save some of the tickets for the next week so that I could still make production when I didn't feel good.

In 1966 I married Kate, my high school sweetheart. After getting married, I came to the realization that I needed a better paying job, so I left Genesco and went looking for employment with the city of Atlanta. My interests took me to the field of working with law enforcement and the corrections officers.

In 1966 we had our first child. It was a boy who we named Kevin. While working with the city, I received an internship to study political science and religion at the University of Georgia. UGA, in my opinion, was a party town. There was a party almost every night. The student body had breakfast and dinner in a different hall than the rest of the students. Maybe that's why the athletes are so much bigger than the average student, but athletes would have a different menu.

One night during police tactical training, the training officer was showing us how to handcuff an individual. The arrangement was three officers trying to handcuff one other officer. That one officer was supposed to resist the amount of force to restrain him. When I saw so many officers getting hurt by these techniques, I knew that I was not going to get my wrist or my fingers broken, so I decided to give my roommate something to think about.

I had arranged a scenario with him. I wanted him to tell the instructor that I was asleep on the training pad. When my name would be called, I would just lay there on the mat, but as I laid there, my roommate did the exact opposite. He said, "He's not asleep officer." What a roommate! LOL Well, I gave no resistance at all to the three officers assigned to attack me. I looked at my instructor and told him that everybody that is being handcuffed does not resist, and I think that's how I got out of that situation and was able to keep from having my body parts broken that day.

After my basic training, I was selected by the city of Atlanta to put my body and face on a very large billboard to advertise the position I held in corrections. They wanted to use this ad to encourage more of the black community to consider having careers in corrections. I guess you could say that I was a poster child. I was one of the first black correctional officers hired by the city of Atlanta. I had no idea that at the time, I was breaking glass ceilings.

I supervised black and white inmates. It was the first time that I had ever supervised a white man and was able to tell him what he could and could not do. It was a strange and eerie feeling for me. I was very proud of the uniform and my badge.

I was at the University of Georgia for about six months. It was because I had my family to take care of, even though my marriage only lasted three years, that I realized that I needed a part time job. I applied with a company called Wells Fargo. I was carrying millions of dollars each and every day. Once we came out of the money vault, it was safety, safety, safety at all times.

There were a couple of occasions that I remember while working as the officer assigned to the back of the armored truck. I would make a bed out of nothing but money. I wanted to know how it felt to sleep on $2,000,000. What a wonderful bed to lay down on. I didn't even need a pillow or a spread, if you get my point.

The Bible says, "When I was a child, I spoke as a child, I understood as a child, I thought as a child: but when I became a man, I put away childish things," (1 Corinthians 13:11). I did childish things. The fighting, cursing, telling lies, shooting craps or dice. But then, after all of that, I felt a metamorphosis happen on the inside of me. This "duck" had realized that he wasn't a duck anymore. He was a "swan" of a man.

Swans show grace and beauty. I had managed to set a new course in my life, and it was exciting. With all my experience, sometimes I would do things that would not be correct. Now, I will try to be correct in most things that I do.

Five years later, I remarried to a wonderful lady by the name of Joe, who gave me my second son, Rocky. I convinced my boss to hire Joe to work the money vault at Wells Fargo.

At some point in time, I quit my job at Wells Fargo. Two years after that, I left my job with the City of Atlanta for a better paying one, this time with a company named Salvatore. They manufactured leather goods such as ladies' pocketbooks and men's belts. Everything was made of genuine leather, no cheap stuff y'all. I was hired as the receiving manager.

As the receiving manager, some of my responsibilities were to view all purchase orders to match with the items that were ordered and take notes of any discrepancies that the company might have.

Around 1972, Salvatore still had placards that read white only for the bathrooms and the water fountain. It was those placards that inspired me to change these conditions on my job.

Remember my opening statement, in a world of many colors of people, I think we are more alike than unalike, well, I wanted my working conditions to change with a quickness, so I joined the union.

Episode 6

– Joining the AFL-CIO

The name of our union was, and still is AFL-CIO. This is one of the largest unions in America. I was advised by other company managers not to join the union because it would be a conflict of interest. After much thought and consideration and prayer, I decided to join anyway.

For the next two years, I was very heavily involved with the union, and I was elected shop steward. A shop steward is a person that officially represents the union on behalf of the employees of the company in regard to any grievances they may have with the company. I was very vocal and passionate about my responsibility as a leader.

Just two years later, I got elected as the president of local #365 in Atlanta. I inherited many problems from the former president. I remember on one occasion, I was asked by the employees and by the local 365 body, to go to New York and try to convince the international president to send them another international representative. Let's call him Mr. Fred.

The local voted to have him removed from office at our local headquarters in Atlanta. I was asked by my local body to go to New York and speak to the president of the international AFL-CIO. We'll call him Mr. Frank.

Once I laid eyes on Mr. Frank after entering his office, I thought to myself that he looked like he was either Jewish or Italian. He was much shorter than I, and I stand at 5 feet 9 inches. He had a long green cigar that he was smoking in my presence. His desk looked like it was made of real marble, and so did his lamps and end tables. His office was located in a very large bank building downtown Manhattan, New York.

My meeting with the president lasted for approximately one hour. For some reason, he would not accept the petition that I was presenting to him from the employees at Salvatore. As a matter of fact, he informed me to go back to Atlanta with what I had. He then showed me his closed fist and said to me, "Like this, you are somebody." Then he took that same fist and held one finger up and said, "But like this, you are nobody."

At this point in our conversation, I began to feel very uncomfortable and threatened by his demonstration and the words that he had used. I came to a crossroads in my mind. What would be my next move? I only had four days to complete my mission.

After much thought and praying to God, I decided to put the petition in the mail. I sent it certified so that someone would have to sign for it. I addressed it to the president of AFL-CIO, Mr. Frank. I was determined to give the concerns of my local union.

At that point, a metaphoric experience changed all my bad things that I went through in my early life. Now the "ugly duck" side of me had transformed into a beautiful swan of a man, who had begun to spread his wings. Life was beginning to go in the opposite direction for me.

Around 1974, when I returned from New York City, it was time for negotiations with our company, Salvatore's. Things weren't going very well for my union. Company management wanted to take more, but only willing to give less than before, so I decided to call a wildcat strike. A wildcat strike is when the local goes out on its own without the help of its' international union.

As life would have it, I was the only union member to come out with a picket sign for several weeks. Remember the quote, "A friend in need is a friend indeed"? Well, I called my best friend Roy E. Ward aka Blue, who came to my aide. He and I walked about four weeks together during that strike. We stopped all trucks and cargo from coming on to Salvatore property. The owner of Salvatore became so uncomfortable that he started coming to work with an Atlanta police officer. I decided to look for outside help for my local union 365, and guess who I found? The Reverend Hosea L. Williams!

At that time, he was president of the Poor People Union in Atlanta, and this was how I met him. Under his leadership and council, I decided to join SCLC, which is an acronym for Southern Christian Leadership Conference. With the help of

Hosea and the Poor People Union, we ended the strike at Salvatore, but the two unions could not save my job. That ended another episode in my life in the Black Mecca of the south, Atlanta.

I remember on one occasion while working for SCLC, Hosea asked me to go to the Atlanta Airport to pick up Mr. Dick Gregory, a close friend and colleague of SCLC. Gregory was a well-known civil rights activist and presidential candidate for the United States. My job was to bring him back to the SCLC office.

In my conversation with him, he gave me his thoughts about the missing and murdered children of Atlanta. He informed me that the majority of the boys were castrated, because some of the doctors and scientists had found a new drug to fight cancer called interferon. He said that one of the ingredients needed to make up interferon is sickle cell, and that cell needed to come from a black adolescent males penis. WOW! What a story!

After much conversation with Mr. Gregory, I came to the realization that this man was a blessed man sent from God. In my opinion, he was in touch with The Lord of this universe. Here is another episode in my life.

Episode 7

– The march to City Hall

round 1975, the members of SCLC, led by Reverend Hosea Williams, formed a coalition of members from the Atlanta chapter. Our plans were to bring attention to the senseless killing of black men who were unarmed when they were shot.

We decided to have a march that was to start from the Atlanta City Jail, which was on Decatur Street, up Albin Avenue, and was to climax at City Hall in downtown Atlanta. I was one of the leaders on that day. Believe it or not, we used the same mule wagon that Dr. King's body was carried on. I was very proud to be a member of that march and demonstration. We had about 300 protestors that day.

During that march, we got ambushed by the Atlanta Police Department. They came from behind buildings on Auburn Avenue on horseback. They had billy clubs, or blackjack sticks, as many people called them. They beat some of us down to the ground. They acted as if they enjoyed every swing of those billy clubs. They also filtrated our march. Some of them were undercover as if they were part of the march, but they had a plot for us.

As we were marching, they were carrying rocks! Their pockets were filled with various sized rocks, big and small which they began to throw up into the air. Everybody would scatter. We had no knowledge of where the rocks were coming from. All of the protestors went to jail on that day. I was charged with criminal trespassing on government property. The government property in question was the Atlanta Police Department. That charge stayed on my police record for 35 years! WOW!

Once I found out about it, I had to go down to Georgia Bureau of Investigations, aka GBI, to have it removed. Now, I set out on a new and exciting life as a swan of a man. During my service with SCLC, I decided to get involved in community service. Here is another episode I'd like to share.

Episode 8

– No more ugly duck

The "Ugly Duck" side of me in my early younger life is all gone now. No more lying, no more fighting, and no more gambling. I had had enough of that duck life. The "Swan" in me took a swan dive into life itself.

It started with a PTA elementary school called Sky Heaven. I was elected as the parliamentarian for the school. Two years later, I was elected as vice president of the school PTA. What a change for me. The metamorphosizing in me had taken over my then present life.

By word of mouth, I obtained a position with the Atlanta Public Schools. I was fortunate enough to get the position as a community liaison. My assignment was to facilitate the concerns of the school to the parents. I was also in charge of school attendance. I would travel from school to school where there was an attendance problem. I became a cub master, and a scout master at Sky Haven Elementary School where my son attended.

After much mediation, I decided that I wanted to throw my hand in the political arena. I was just trying to give something back to my community that had given so much to me. My first adventure was to try for the Atlanta City Council. That didn't go very well, but I learned and gained a lot of experience from being a candidate. My platform was built around law and order. Wow, does that sound familiar?

Today, what goes around comes around, there's nothing new under the sun. Two years later, I threw my hand into the Atlanta School Board race. My platform there was the same as it was with the Atlanta City Council, law, and order.

As you can see, I was a very busy man in the 70's. Oh, by the way, I lost both races, but acquired a vast amount of knowledge and experience in politics. One of the things that I learned was that the rich controlled politics and the politicians, and the politicians controlled the people. Sad, but from my experience, quite true.

Also, in the decade of the seventies, it became a time for me to be more in contact with God. My walk with God was more defined than ever after teaching Sunday school for over 30 years at Beulah Baptist Church. This church, Beulah Baptist, was the place that I was raised up in as a pew member. I had a phenomenal experience with the spirit of God. This was in the late 70's. He allowed me to feel His presence. It was an out-of-body experience like when Jesus asked His disciples to have faith in Him when He was walking on the water. In my vision, I was also walking on the water. I was afraid to take that one step, and when I did, I became a new soldier for God Almighty.

After teaching Sunday school for all those years, God, and Pastor Reverend E. D. Thomas, who was the pastor of Beulah Baptist Church at that time, called me to the ministry of The Lord. I was still working with SCLC part time.

Episode 9

– Hello Sid and Marty

My next episode was with a company called Sid and Marty Krofft. It was a downtown amusement park located in the Omni Hotel. It was owned by two brothers, Sid and Marty, who were professional puppeteers. They had a television show called H.R. Pufnstuf. This show came on every Saturday morning in Atlanta.

I was hired as a security officer for the amusement park. Our uniforms were like those of Bobbies, which is what the British call their police officers in England. We were about forty officers strong. Only three of us were black.

On one occasion, we had a company picnic going down the Hooch, aka the Chattahoochee River. As we arrived at the banks of the Hooch, we were ready to party. We filled an empty raft with about seven cases of beer and three gallons of alcohol on that day. I noticed that we didn't have enough life jackets or enough inner tubes to go around our waists for safety. Officer Jackson and Officer Earwin and myself were the three black officers that I mentioned earlier in this story. This presented us with what I called the perfect storm.

Officer Jackson and I got into a kerfuffle about the last inner tube on that day. Officer Jackson out tussled me for the last inner tube. He was the type of person that when he was drinking alcohol, he would pass out after three drinks. Well, the decision for me was quite clear. Fact is, I knew that I couldn't swim, and the water was ice cold on that day, so I told the rest of the officers, "Y'all go ahead and have a good time but leave me a six pack. I will wait here on the banks of the Hooch."

I decided to take a sun bath because of the melanin in my skin. Well, about two hours later, the white officers came back screaming at me saying that Jackson fell out of the raft and they could not find him. I went back with them to search for Jackson. The Atlanta Fire and Rescue Team found his body tied up by roots from a tree. Just think, if I would have won the kerfuffle or tussle with Jackson about the last inner tube, that could have been me instead of him.

When we went back to work the next day, management kept the news teams away from me and the other black officer. Then they commenced to firing me and the other black officer for frivolous reasons and without just cause. One of the next episodes comes after losing my job with Sid and Marty Krofft amusement park.

Episode 10

– Goodbye Sid and Marty

My next employment adventure was with the Atlanta Public Schools. I was hired as a school administrator. My position was school community liaison officer. My first school assignment was at East Lake Elementary School and Murphy High School.

The year was about 1979. My responsibility was the issue of truancy in both schools and to also work with parents and teachers to resolve conflict resolution in our schools. That sounds familiar to this very day.

One of my absentee students was named Lubie Geter. He was one of Atlanta's missing and murdered children. I believe my first encounter with him was at East Lake Elementary School, and then later at Murphy High School. These two schools were assigned to me. This was all so long ago.

I remember every night when the news came on at ten o'clock. The first comment was, it's ten o'clock, do you know where your child is? Wow, what a comment to have to make to its' viewers.

Our kids were coming up missing and murdered. They were all black boys. Authorities found their bodies lying around express ways, the Chattahoochee River, and also in woods located in Atlanta. One body was found behind a gas station. His body was mutilated, over and over again. It was a bad and sad time for black parents in the city of Atlanta.

Reverend Hosea Williams was president of SCLC Atlanta chapter at that time. Paths crossing again: Remember Reverend S. T. Huff? He was the rent man that I mentioned earlier in my story, who used to make it rain nickels, dimes, and quarters every Friday afternoon. I hadn't seen him since I was a child. Our paths crossed again when I became a young man.

One day while I was shopping in South Dekalb Mall in the early 80's, I was going into the mall, and he was coming out. It was I who recognized him first. Once I introduced myself to him, we both cried. He and I did a lot of reminiscing. I informed him that I had also become a man of the cloth. Paths crossing for the last time.

Reverend Huff was a Methodist minister, and I was a Baptist minister, which was two different denominations. At that time, I was still preaching and teaching Sunday School, and had for many, many decades. As time passed by, I could feel the gravity and compelling nature of this powerful man of God. He convinced me to come to his church and preach at least once a month. WOW! This lasted about two years.

A time came when he and his wife planned a vacation trip to Mexico. He informed me that he was very apprehensive about flying on an airplane. It would be his very first time. The day after arriving in Mexico, they went on a sightseeing tour in Mexico City. They were on the tour bus when he told his wife that he decided not to get off the bus at that stop. He wanted to stay on the bus, so everyone got off the bus, including his wife. He told them that he would wait there for them.

When everyone arrived back from the walking tour and got back on the bus, that's when Mrs. Huff found him slumped over in the seat that he was sitting in. After closer observation, it was determined that he had had a heart attack. May God rest the soul of my friend and confidant, Reverend S. T. Huff.

Episode 11

– New kid on the block

The episodes of my life continue turning again and again. Now I'm off on a new career working for the state of Georgia as a correctional officer. More specifically, a CO2. In corrections, officers are either CO1, CO2, or sergeant. I started out for the state as a corrections officer because of my experience with the city of Atlanta.

On my very first day I was assigned to work in the cafeteria of the institution. I was so new that I had not been given a uniform. I had to work in my street clothes that day. I had a very difficult time as you can imagine. The inmates gave me no respect because they knew that I was the new kid on the block. They gave me no respect at all. Imagine that. If I asked an inmate to stop, he would keep walking. If I asked one to turn left, he would turn right, just to give you a couple of examples of my very first day on the job.

After feeding time was over, my assignment was to work in a building called D building. Some inmates called it "the hole". It was also called the building for the criminally insane, wow. None of the officers who had any seniority would work in this building.

As life would have it, this would be my training ground for the days to come. I had to use a strait jacket on the inmates from time to time. I had to learn how to properly place this jacket on an inmate. The jacket was used to restrain an inmate from physical harm to himself or anyone else. I worked in the building on the second shift for about four years.

One night an inmate decided to have an arranged scenario while he was locked down in the hole for an institution violation. He decided that he did not want to be locked down anymore. This particular inmate was a golden glove boxing champion at Metro C I.

He started a fire in his prison cell that night. There was only one officer on duty at the time. That officer opened the cell door to put the fire out and that started the arranged scenario for his escape.

The inmate started to beat the officer with those trained boxing hands of destruction. After he finished beating him with his fist, he kicked the officer over and over again until the officer passed out. This inmate beat him this bad because the officer would not relinquish the keys for his escape.

After his escape, we looked for this inmate for about two weeks. I was on stakeout duty across the street in a cemetery where he used to live. The way we apprehended him was by a tip from a cab driver who had heard of the escape. The inmate needed a way to move around in the city of Atlanta and it was this cab driver that provided the service. After much conversation, the driver keyed up his mic, or left his mic on, and that's how we apprehended the inmate. We got our man.

About a year later, I was elected as president of the Correction Officers Association in Atlanta. I was also promoted to the rank of sergeant almost simultaneously. The other Association group of officers was called the Fraternal Order of Police.

One group was all white, and the other group was all black. Imagine that y'all.

I remember another incident that happened at Metro C I where I had an encounter with an inmate. We will call him Rick. Rick had also arranged a scenario. He decided on his own that he wanted to be moved to another institution close to his hometown so that his family would visit him more.

One day, Rick plotted to have himself removed from the prison. He obtained a razor blade and began to cut his arm over and over again. He took some of his blood and drew a sickle and crescent moon on the wall in his cell. I was told by a mason fraternity brother that someone had shown him this sign. You would use it if you were in distress or needed help.

On that day, Rick received a visit from the warden of the prison. The warden asked Rick if he could come into his cell and Rick's reply was, "Sure, you're a man just like I am. Come on in.", but the warden decided that it was not in his best interest to enter that cell. Then the captain came down to the cell and asked Rick if he could come into his cell. Rick's reply, once again, was "Sure, you're a man just like I am. Come on in." There again, the captain decided that it was not in his best interest to go into the cell that day. So, then I asked Rick if I could come in and he gave me the same reply that he had given the warden and the captain. I entered his cell and I consulted with him for two hours about his conditions at Metro C I. After an hour of conversation, he gave me the razor. About two weeks later he was moved to another prison.

As president of the Atlanta chapter of the correction officer association, part of my responsibility was to provide security for over seven hundred inmates and staff members. I was also allowed to travel from my institution to many other institutions throughout the state of Georgia as their representative for the correction officer association.

As president, my job was to collect grievances from the black officers complaining about promotions and disparity in treatment. The white officers did not like talking to me about their grievances when I approached them. Part of my responsibility was to report the grievances to the commissioner of rehabilitation of the state of Georgia.

Another aspect of my responsibility at Metro C.I., and the most challenging part of the day, was called count time. We had to know where all seven hundred inmates were at a particular time of day. No inmates could move around in the institution until all of them were accounted for by the shift supervisor. It was like playing that game called Simon Says, only this was not a game at all. This was real life.

When all of the inmates were accounted for by the shift supervisor, he or she would get on the intercom and give what we called a clear count, and all activity for the inmates would resume.

Now, back to the grievance issues from the line officers. My job was to effectively communicate their concerns to the commissioner of rehabilitation for the state of Georgia. The commissioner was not too receptive of me bringing him the complaint from the black officers about the white officers being promoted over them when the black officers had more seniority.

As a result of my concern for the matter, about one year later, I was investigated by the office of internal affairs for the State of Georgia. About six months after that, I was demoted from a sergeant back to a corrections officer 2. For some reason, the warden of the institution did not want me within the confines of the prison.

With all of my experience, they did not want me there. They gave me added assignments such as working what we called 16 P, which was the perimeter assignment. The other one was working in the tower of the institution. 16 P was a job that none of the regular officers were willing to work. You have to be in the truck for 8 hours driving around, and around, and around the entire perimeter of the facility.

By me working on the outside of the prison, that kept me away from the line officers that I was sworn to help in their times of need. So, I filed a lawsuit for racial discrimination by my superiors. I could not afford an attorney, therefore I had to learn how to practice law on my own and I did it pretty well.

The State of Georgia tried to have the case dismissed. They said it was a frivolous case, but the judge said, "No, I don't think it's a frivolous case. As a matter of fact, I'm going to appoint him a United States Attorney." Once it got into federal court, my attorney failed me by not filing motions on time and that was the end of that story in Corrections. I lost by default.

In the beginning of my venture, I was terrified when I saw the paperwork that read Jerome Carithers versus the state of Georgia. WOW, I think I was bamboozled and hoodwinked by my attorney.

Episode 12

– Racial discrimination

During this episode in my life, I was feeling very alone and ostracized by this experience, but life goes on. My story is not about rags to riches, but about a man who thought he was a lame duck, and as life went on, found that he had metamorphosized into a new being. Finding out that life had turned him, me, into a swan of a man.

Now, to a child who thought he was the ugly duck in his family, with none of his siblings having the same skin color or the same hair texture, my thinking process was much different them theirs. I had no idea what life had in store for me. With all of my life experiences, I became a swan. I got involved in community service affairs.

Around 1982, I was called into the ministry by the African Methodist Church as a pastor of New Haven in Griffin, Georgia. Also, that same year, I decided to become a candidate for the

Atlanta City Council. My call to the church and becoming a candidate for the ACC, almost happened at the same time. It was then that I decided that I had made a very foolish decision.

Just after one year, I resigned at New Haven Methodist Church. My thought process was, I believed that I could help more people as a city councilman than being a pastor of a church. I wanted very badly to become councilman of post number five. It was the same post, or the same area that I grew up in as a child and young man. This would have been a dream come true for me.

If you will recall early in my story, I mentioned the communities of Reynoldstown, Edgewood, Kirkwood, and Cabbagetown. After I qualified for the seat of the 5th district, I started to walk the area in which I was trying to see and low and behold I was able to understand how general gentrification had set in all of these settlements.

With all my life training experiences, I know it prepared me one more time for what I was truly seeking: public service for all the people, but life goes on.

I remember around 1990, one of my favorite recording artists was Curtis Mayfield. I heard him speak on an interview after one of his songs, A New World Order, and in that interview, he was asked, "Curtis, how do you make hit after hit?" And his reply was that life had always been his script and I said to myself, boy do I have a script to write. That was my first inclination to start writing a book.

Somewhere in between that, Hosea Williams said to me one day, "You should write a book about your life. I don't understand how you made it this far." I admired this man very much. That was my second inspiration to write a book about my life. I believe I have had at least 23 job changes in my life. WOW!

Moving right along with my life, the swan of the man takes flight again. I lost my bid for the Atlanta City Council. About two years later, I decided to run for the Atlanta School Board post number 7, which was a citywide post, meaning all over Atlanta, Georgia.

I really wanted to be a public servant to all of the citizens of Atlanta. I kissed a lot of babies while juggling between the city council post and the school board seat. My platform for both of these seats were conflict resolution, and law, and order.

I learned in my lifetime that what goes around comes around. In the late 80's and early 90's, I was being asked by a television station reporter, in reference to the school board seat, what would I do to stop so much violence and the breaking into our schools. My response was by putting metal detectors in all schools, also putting chains on the locks as well. By doing that, other people could not come into the school who weren't there for school, but for other purposes.

Well, back in those days, it was not a popular statement, but as I said, what goes around comes around. Now everybody wants metal detectors. I guess I was a little bit ahead of my time, even back then, wow, but look at today's society.

Somewhere in my walk of life, I went to the federal penitentiary to council an inmate who had been locked up for many years. When a man has time on his hands, sometimes God will visit him, and this inmate made this remark to me. "Reverend does the Bible explain and say that the world will be destroyed by fire this time?" and I said, "yes". Then he asked me, "what about gunfire?" What a thought to have.

In 1992 I started my own transportation company. The business was very successful. It allowed me to go on vacation for the very first time out of the United States.

I will never forget my first client, her name was Ann. She was a blind lady who I transported five days a week. She also had cancer. She was very hard to get along with because of all the medication that she was on all the time, but I needed people to transport, and she needed to be transported. In other words, I needed her, and she needed me.

When the hospital released her to me, they gave me no instructions on how to get her home. Ann was not always blind. She remembered the streets and landmarks in Gwinnett County. Because I did not know the terrain in another county, every morning we would get in a kerfuffle because of all of that medication that she was on each and every day of her life. But when I after picking her up each day and evening, we became friends. We would go to lunch and talk about our differences. About a year later, Ann passed away. At her funeral, her mother mentioned me several times during her service. What a friend Ann was.

On one of my trips out of the country, I went to Mexico. It was interesting to find out how other countries looked and felt in comparison to mine. It was quite a shock to see people driving on the opposite side of their cars as opposed to what I was used to seeing in America, as well as speaking a language different than what I'm used to hearing, wow.

I found out that I like to see other cultures in life. The food I ate was quite interesting to me. Always take your water if you go out of the country, that's just a suggestion that I have, and also, have the correct change. For some reason they're always out of change. It's just part of their culture, if you get my drift.

On another trip out of this country, I traveled to Montego Bay, Jamaica, where the spoken language is called patois. It is a mix of creole and

English put together. Jamaica also has what is called a rainforest there, and their beach is made of reef which comes from the bottom of the beach; therefore, it is not man made.

Jamaica is famed as the birthplace of Reggae music and rum punch. The bottle reads overproof rum. If I was a native American, I would call it fire water! I went to a part of Montego Bay called the Old Country which was over the old mountains. I experienced the natives cooking out of the ground. That was fascinating to me. Their musical instruments were made from household equipment. For example, rub board and wash pots. I noticed that in Jamaica the ground was black as opposed to Georgia red clay. That's a part of my story traveling outside of America.

Episode 13

– Three strikes, I'm out

About two years later after my vacation, I bought a home in Clarkston, Georgia. The population there was about 5,000 people. The city slogan was little city with a big heart. I found out at some point that it was the most ethnically diverse city within a mile in America.

Most of the population, or residents, were black, but they were all refugees for the most part. I learned that when you are a refugee, you do not have voting privileges. This is one way the few controlled the many in this city. This is what some people would call a good old boys' town, including myself. The white families that lived in this city had good family values and connections and control of what went on in this city. Remember the slogan "The little city with a big heart." Wow.

In this little city, Jim Crow was alive and doing very well. In the late 90's, I decided to test the political waters in this little city called Clarkston. I decided to become a candidate for councilman.

I remember on one occasion, I was invited to Meet the Candidates night. On that night, I brought up very sensitive matters about the city policies and procedures. This made the powers to be very uncomfortable. I had always been one who was attracted to good trouble. Believe me when I say to you that whites held a firm grip on the city that I'm talking about, "The little city with a big heart." I lost that councilman seat by 14 votes.

After the election, some of the politicians and some of the residents decided they wanted me completely out of Clarkston, and I do mean that literally. They wanted me out really bad.

I remember that I used to always cut my grass on a Saturday. One Sunday morning I was preparing to go to church. As I began to walk down my driveway, I spotted a hog's head sitting on a plate in my front yard. The whole hog's head! Burning incense were stuck in the flesh of the head. I was shocked! I could not believe what I was looking at. That was my first inclination that someone meant business with me.

About two weeks later, as usual, I was on my way to church. As I approached my car, down on my lawn I saw a large white bag that really intimidated me. I picked up a stick to see what was in the bag. I wanted to know, and I did not want to know.

I called the Clarkston Police Department to give them the information about the large white bag and asked them to come out and investigate. They never called me back. I called them again and they reported to me that there were three dead chicken hawks in that bag. I was traumatized about all these bad feeling towards me. That was strike two for me.

Strike three came under the same circumstances but instead of a hog head or chicken hawks, I found six 38 caliber bullets standing up in my driveway. I never found out who was responsible for those three incidents that happened at my home in Clarkston. And as the phrase goes, "three strikes and you are out," so I was out of Clarkston. There's another phrase that goes, "you have to know when to hold them and know when to fold them," so it was time for me to fold them and I moved out of Clarkston.

About three years later, my youngest son went back to Clarkston to buy an automobile. He is my Jr., so he has the same name as I do. My son told me that the car salesperson had said that a lot of the residents there were glad when his father moved out of their little city with the big heart.

It was around the year 2000 while working a part time job in downtown Atlanta that I met a poet by the name of Yann, who was visiting here from California at the time. She said to me, "Tell me something about Atlanta, Georgia." I told her about Stone Mountain, Grant Park, Six Flags, our State Capital, and many more sites in Atlanta. I didn't know that as we were having this conversation, she was writing a poem about me. She named it FREE TIME.

It read . . . "Dear Saint Jerome, when you take the time to smell the flowers you see them. You Saint Jerome with your magic eyes are playing piano melodies with your true soothing stories of your

Georgia life." Now as for me, I had never heard of a Saint Jerome or understood why she would compare me to such a person.

A couple of years later, I did some research about Saint Jerome, also known as Jerome of Stridon. He was a Christian priest. He translated many biblical texts from Hebrew, Aramaic, and Greek into Latin, and is considered a doctor of the church. I know that I am not a saint, but I believe we have some of the same characteristics. I am a Doctor of Divinity.

Old father time was beginning to call me a senior citizen and I began to wonder who would hire me since I spent most of my adult life in good trouble. Good trouble such as being a civil rights activist, union president, candidate for the Atlanta City Council and the Atlanta school Board. Well, to answer the question as to who would hire me, I found employment with the transportation department. There, I found myself a job driving a school bus. Some of the benefits were health insurance, life insurance, paid holidays, and personal days off. Just what I needed.

My first day on the job behind the wheel my driving trainer said to me that I was not catching on fast enough for her during my training period. She was so disgusted with me as a potential driver that she left me on the school bus by myself. Another trainer was assigned to me and that was how I became a school bus driver.

After driving buses for about two years, I was called in the office by the manager to see if I was interested in becoming a driver trainer. My answer was yes. I liked being a trainer and meeting new potential drivers. Look at how God will work things out.

About three years later, I was promoted to become the trainer for all the new drivers. I was in the classroom teaching all drivers new and old. This was one of my wow moments in life. To make a long story short, I worked my way up, literally. The transportation department for the Board of Education.

My next social climb was to become the transportation dispatcher for all 500 buses that traveled through the city of Atlanta. We had a very high turnover in this department. All of this happened in about ten years. My last promotion was terminal manager, and that was as high as you could go in that field that I worked in. I was in charge of firing and hiring. I was in charge of all personnel that worked in the transportation department for the school buses for the City of Atlanta.

After about seven years, I resigned from that position because of too much stress at my age. Remember the Ugly Duck of a man who found that he was a Swan of a man was innate in me.

In 2009, I had multiple strokes caused by high blood pressure. Imagine that y'all. Three strokes to be exact. For a short period of time, I could not talk or walk straight. It hurt not to be able to walk or talk. Something that we take for granted on a daily basis all the time. I once cried about my circumstances for many days. Not because of any pain, but because of my inability to communicate.

One night while I was hospitalized, I began to pray to The Lord of the Universe. My prayer was, Lord, if I cannot talk, I cannot teach Sunday school or preach. Three days later, He gave me all of my strength, my ability to talk and think better than I was before.

Now that I am a senior citizen, I still have the ability to help other people which is my calling in life. For I am a lover and not a fighter, I am a giver and not a taker.

Episode 14

– Thanks President Obama

With all my life experiences, I was blessed enough to get other employment working in the school system. This time though, it was at the Andrew Young YMCA Learning Academy out on Campbellton Road. I was hired as a volunteer worker. It had always been my life's joy to work with my kids, and other people's kids. It's not work when I'm performing this duty. It's a calling I think God put on me.

After working for about six years with the jump program, I received an accommodation letter from the President of the United States. This accommodation was for my volunteer work. It is called the President's Volunteer Service Award for the Year of 2013. This letter has the President's seal at the top of it. As I looked and saw the seal of the eagle, the bald eagle, I realized that now the Ugly

Duck is soaring with the eagles of life thanks to President Barack Obama.

www.ingramcontent.com/pod-product-compliance
Lightning Source LLC
Chambersburg PA
CBHW060747260726
48660CB00002B/508